Out, damned spot!

Preserving your personal
papers and memorabilia

Gráinne Doran

Wexford County Council Public Library Service, 2002

Published by Wexford County Council
Public Library Service, Wexford

© Wexford Public Library Service September 2002

ISBN: 0-9519800-7-6

Design by Third Eye Graphics
Printed by C&R Print

Table of contents

Foreword

Nearly every home has its store of important memorabilia. They may include certificates of births and deaths, examination records, licences and deeds relating to property. There may be old farm or other business ledgers, school reports, maps, diaries. Some people have a strong sense of family history and retain papers and mementoes that mark important occasions in the life of the family and its members. These may be medals, videos of anniversary celebrations, letters from family or friends from long ago or far away. Whatever the range they are kept because they are important for a variety of reasons. They may be stored away in a file, a drawer, or in a cardboard box in the bottom of the wardrobe.

Family archives reveal how families change and grow. They provide evidence for the how, the when and the why of decisions or events that have formed people's lifestyles and possibly their contributions to local and national developments. The material retained can offer an interesting insight over time into a family's values and preoccupations.

Family archives also contribute to community identity and heritage. Many of County Wexford's local history publications owe their authority in part at least to the access their researchers have been granted to family archive collections. These can be a unique primary source for social or economic history.

The popularity of family history research in County Wexford both encourages and reinforces the importance of retaining personal records. It also illustrates the range of materials that can offer family history information and the pleasure we get from the examination of whimsical treasures as well as from more formal legal documents.

For all these reasons, Wexford County Council has published this introductory guide to maintaining personal or family records at home. It answers the many questions that re-occur when people tackle the care and preservation of old documents and other memorabilia. A common-sense approach has been adopted. We hope the guide will assist many Wexford people in improving the condition of their family records. We hope also that it may encourage others to start developing collections now that may bring insight and interest in 21st century Wexford to future generations.

Councillor Lorcan Allen
Chairman
Wexford County Council

Seamus Dooley
County Manager
Wexford County Council

September 2002

Acknowledgements

The author would like to thank the following individuals for assistance in compiling this booklet:

Preservation Equipment Limited, Norfolk, England for permission to use illustrations from their Sourcebook.

Rev. J.L. Kehoe, Helen Skrine, the Hughes, and Donald MacDonald for the inclusion of illustrative material from their collections, and Eithne Scallan and David Rowe for their dedicated efforts in sourcing interested parties.

Fionnuala Hanrahan, County Librarian, Rita O'Brien, Executive Librarian and Celestine Rafferty, Local Studies Manager, Wexford County Council Public Library Service, for their invaluable advice and editorial assistance.

To all who maintain personal collections, I hope that you may glean some practical advice from this booklet and that your efforts will nurture a desire in others to contribute to our cultural legacy.

Gráinne Doran
Archivist, Wexford
County Council
Public Library
Service

Introduction

We all have documents in our possession that evoke fond memories of a bygone era, a loved one or a trip down memory lane. Whether we treasure these items for their sentimental value or their material worth, can we really guarantee that they will last indefinitely under present storage conditions?

Our homes may be fraught with dangers for our precious keepsakes unless we adopt and adhere to the correct environmental and storage conditions.

This booklet addresses the preservation of family treasures in the home and alerts owners to the detrimental effects occasioned on their collections by a range of factors.

It is by no means definitive and the author acknowledges that paper-based items take precedence over artefacts. Common sense advice is given in the form of helpful guidelines for promoting the longevity of collections, while advice of a specialist nature is included for the serious collector on the

DUBLIN, WICKLOW AND WEXFORD RAILWAY. EXPRESS ENGINE No. 58.
By The Locomotive Publishing Company, Ltd., London.

range of suitable archival quality storage materials. Proper storage and handling of items can be relatively inexpensive, and can lead to future savings by reducing the need for repair of materials. Preservation can be costly and it may be necessary to measure the costs in accordance with the intrinsic worth or value of items. Where material is particularly fragile, it is advisable to consult a professional conservator who can advise on restorative treatments. A list of suppliers of archival products and sundries is given in Appendix 1.

The future of any community is unthinkable without documentary evidence of its past, and this is reflected in the burgeoning interest in family history research. Researching and maintaining a personal archive serves to foster a sense of pride in a family's history and, as an inherent part of our local heritage, such materials should be adequately protected and preserved. However, future generations must not lose sight of their role in supplementing and safeguarding these treasures.

What constitutes our treasures?

Items of a personal nature can encompass a wide range of materials. Although the majority of family heirlooms are paper-based, they can also be generated on other media including photographs, maps, slides, microfilm, audio and visual and more recently, on computer readable storage media. Below are some of the more common keepsakes:

Photos & photo albums

Newspaper cuttings

Family letters

Scrapbooks

Diaries

Ephemera
e.g. postcards, memory cards

Maps

Certificates
e.g. birth cert, diplomas

Genealogy / family history research

Employment references,
incl. curricula vitae

Artefacts,
e.g. coins, jewellery, fabrics

Records / cassettes / videos

Factors undermining preservation

Environmental and storage conditions can have a decisive effect on the preservation of collections, and these conditions are even more difficult to monitor in a domestic setting.

LIGHT

Light is a very potent source of energy and overexposure of documents to visible radiation emitted by windows can result in their rapid ageing and deterioration. The harmful effects of artificial or day light can be prevented by using boxes and drawers to store materials.

DUST

Dust particles over a long period can attract mould growth if warm damp conditions prevail.

HEAT

Undue exposure to heat can result in dry, brittle documents which can be extremely fragile to handle.

DAMP

Mildew can thrive in damp conditions. Staining by mould and foxing are increased with humidity (foxing appears in the form of reddish-brown spots on paper which is thought to be caused by the presence of trace metal in the paper).

INSECT INFESTATION

Many household insects, otherwise regarded as relatively harmless in the domestic environment, can cause irreversible damage to paper-based items. Insects such as silverfish can attack document containers and bore through volumes.

USAGE AND HANDLING

Over-handling of materials can result in grubby documents while the use of inks and pens to mark items can damage them irreparably. Furthermore, placing anything on or leaning on volumes while taking notes can occasion irreversible damage to the spine.

UNSUITABLE STORAGE

The poor quality of storage materials can further degrade family heirlooms, which when combined with fluctuating temperatures, high humidity and atmospheric pollutants (dust, excessive light) can speed up the process of deterioration.

ENVIRONMENTAL CONDITIONS

Physical damage can occur to documents in the presence of high humidity and in an excessively dry atmosphere. Excessive humidity can soften papers and dilute certain inks, in addition to favouring the development of mould.

QUALITY OF ORIGINAL MATERALS

The poor quality of original materials is also responsible for
the degradation of our heirlooms and artefacts. With paper-
based material in particular, the quality of paper has
deteriorated in recent years, and this is most apparent in
newspaper print, which is high in acid content and ages
quite quickly.

Traditionally, some writing inks and other pigments were
highly acidic and susceptible to damage by light. Iron gall ink,
used for centuries, was found to be much too corrosive,
sometimes burning its way through the paper.

So what measures can you take?

A number of simple precautions can be easily adopted to safeguard personal materials, thereby reducing the need for costly treatment work in the future.

- Store items in a stable, dry environment with clean air and good circulation, with minimum exposure to light, dust, heat and damp. The central part of the home provides a safer storage environment for family heirlooms than either a warm attic or a damp basement.

- Damage prevention can be achieved through sound hygiene and control of temperature and humidity.

- Preventative conservation is ongoing and involves the careful removal of paper fasteners, rusty clips and staples from documents and their replacement with inert plastic paper clips. Care should be taken where documents have been tied with string or rubber bands, as the ties may have eaten through the top and bottom papers.

- DO NOT attempt to remove sellotape from documents, particularly if those documents constitute family heirlooms. This work should only be undertaken by a paper conservator who will professionally remove the tape and the underlying sticky residue.

7

- Clean hands and surfaces are paramount. Surface dust can be removed gently from materials with a soft brush or cloth. Before any surface cleaning is undertaken, it is vital to ensure that the document or item is dry. If damp, the likelihood is that dirt and grime will be smeared across it.

- Care should be exercised when handling fragile materials, particularly in relation to photographs and individual documents.

- Soft lead pencils should be used when annotating documents. With regard to photographs, a felt-tip film marking pen can be used on the back of the photo to record the origin of the item (this can be purchased through your local art store).

- Avoid laminating as the process permanently alters items.

- Always unfold documents, as creases can cause long-term marking as can incorrect storage. If unfolding may result in damage to the item, advice should be sought from a conservator.

Storage advice for specific materials

Paper

Paper is inherently unstable due to a high percentage of lignin in its composition, and storage conditions are extremely important as a result.

- Diaries and volumes of value should be wrapped in tissue paper (preferably acid-free), covered with a book sleeve or placed in a polyester pocket, whichever is the most appropriate option for the format, and stored in a box. Wrapping volumes will ensure that they are protected against the deteriorating influences of dust, light, moisture, insects and human handling.

- Family papers should be stored in appropriately-sized enclosures, which will provide physical protection as well as guarding from light and dust.

- An inexpensive method of protecting postcards and other ephemeral material is to store them in economical polyethylene postcard protectors.

- Certificates and employment references should be carefully copied and put in safe storage in folders. Any further copies required should be taken from the duplicate. It is important to ensure that the duplicates are kept apart from the originals.

- Thermal fax papers are very unstable because of their poor quality paper. It is recommended that faxes containing important information be copied onto more durable paper.

- Recommended storage conditions for paper-based items: 13-18 °C and 55-65% RH (Relative Humidity)

Newspapers

Acid is one of the prime enemies of paper and this manifests itself especially in newspapers, causing them to yellow quite rapidly, more particularly when exposed to light.

- Newspaper cuttings and other inferior quality papers should be stored separately to valuable documents.

- If newspapers or clippings are valued most for the information they contain, rather than as artefacts, copying the information on to a more permanent quality paper should be undertaken.

- If the original paper needs to be retained, a sheet of buffered acid-free tissue paper should be interleaved between the pages to reduce the risk of acid migration and the item stored flat in a suitable container. Alternatively, if a single cutting warrants permanent retention, it can be placed in an inert polyester pocket or envelope, thereby cutting down significantly on over-handling. It is worth remembering that photocopies will far outlive newsprint when stored under normal conditions.

- Newspaper cuttings pasted into scrapbooks are not designed to last permanently, as the adhesive used to paste the cuttings eventually seeps through, thereby clouding the text. The best solution is to purchase a ring binder with polyester pockets.

Photographs

The method you employ to assemble scrapbooks and photograph albums can either enhance the preservation of the items or cause irreparable results. Photographs are one of the most sensitive documents to preserve in a personal collection, and it is worth remembering that what may be appropriate for everyday disposable snapshots may not be suitable for photos designated as family keepsakes.

- Photographs should be stored in the coolest and driest spot in the home – colour photographs in particular are inherently unstable and go through a gradual fading process, so it is imperative that they do not come into direct contact with sunlight.

- The recommended type of photo album for valued photos is one with plastic pocket pages. This has the advantage that no adhesive is needed to secure the photos. Self-stick pages provide their own means of securing photos to the page, but they surround the items with adhesive which can be detrimental in the long-term.

- In general, plastic pages and cover sheets made from uncoated pure polyethylene and polyester (also called mylar) are considered stable and non-damaging to photographs, unlike PVC enclosures which can cause deterioration of items over time.

- As an alternative to polyester, non-acidic, lignin-free paper pages with plastic cover sheets protect photographs from fingerprints, accidental spills and prevent the photographs from sticking to each other in damp conditions.

- If preserving individual photographs, each item should be stored in its own separate polyester pocket or envelope and stored horizontally. Static electricity attracts dust, causing scratches on photographic materials, especially films, so it is paramount that they are stored in enclosures. These transparent envelopes permit viewing of items without direct handling.

- The most cost-effective method of accommodating photographs when using a ring binder album is to purchase a variety of single, two-pocket and four-pocket polyester pages.

- Glass plate negatives should only be held at the edges in order to ensure their physical protection. Each plate should be placed in individual acid-free enclosures (emulsion side facing down) and stored vertically in a suitable document box.

- In order to ensure that original photographs are protected from over-handling, a laser copy can be taken. By duplicating, the size can be enhanced and the quality can be significantly upgraded.

- Ensure that framed pictures or photographs mounted on walls are not in the direct line of sunlight. It is worth investing in tinted glass which will significantly cut down on over-exposure to light.

- An important tip to remember when preserving photographs is to source each item, including such details as subject (place or persons) and date. This may seem purposeless to you now, but think of the difficulty family members may experience in the next generation when trying to identify such people or events. When annotating photographs, always ensure that the item is placed on a hard surface. Use a felt-tip film marking pen and write lightly on the back of the item, taking care to allow the ink to dry before storing items.

- Recommended storage conditions for photographs: 10-15 °C and 30-40% RH

Records / cassettes / video tapes / sound recordings

- Keep records in their sleeves and cassettes in their cases when not in use, safeguarding them from undue exposure to dust particles. For particularly valuable record collections, anti-static sleeves made from polyethylene can be purchased which will reduce the attraction of dust. Alternatively, records can be placed in acid-free storage sleeves and stored vertically in custom-made record storage boxes.

- Records should only be handled on the edges.

- Tape surfaces should NEVER be touched – if a tape has become tangled, necessitating handling, cotton gloves should be worn.

- Acid-free audio cassette storage boxes can be obtained which can hold individual cassettes in their original cases, with a lid to protect from light and dust.

- Recommended storage conditions for sound recordings: 7-13 °C and 40-60% RH

Non-documentary materials

Non-documentary material comprises a wide range of family artefacts, including coins, medals, seals and fabrics.

- NEVER store non-documentary items in direct juxtaposition with documents as the acid or corrosive quality of the metal artefact could transfer onto the documents.

- Maps can present a preservation challenge because of their size. They should be kept flat if at all possible and stored in an appropriately-sized folder.

- Artefacts should be placed in little memorabilia acid-free boxes.

- For storage of fabric items, wrap in acid-free tissue paper and store in an appropriately-sized container, preferably a corrugated textile storage box.

- Seals are vulnerable, especially where they are pendant from a document. Made from wax, shellac or metal, they can become dirty and grimy in a short time due to over-handling and incorrect storage. When surface cleaning wax seals, care should be exercised due to the fragility of the items, and dust should be brushed off gently. Seals made from shellac are hardier and can withstand a reasonably strong brush.

Electronic Records

Technology is now increasingly used as an adjunct to genealogical and local history research. One of the main benefits is its ability to digitise images, which can in turn be printed out, e-mailed or incorporated into a web page.

- A clean, dust-free environment is strongly recommended for electronic records.

- Scanning is particularly suitable for valuable photographs, as the digitized image can be used over and over without disturbing the original.

- For the long-term care of CDs, it is advisable to store them in acid-free archival quality CD storage envelopes, which have a protective flap.

- An important point to remember when working on your family database or related research is to regularly back-up your work. Ensure that there is a box of disks to hand so that you remember to back-up your work at the end of each day. Technology can be temperamental and it is not worth losing a morning's work just for the sake of those extra few minutes. The usual format to save to is the floppy disk, but where images are employed, saving onto CD-ROM is more productive. It is worth remembering that the longevity of any electronic medium cannot be guaranteed, so it is

advisable to print out your work regularly and dispose of previous drafts where necessary.

- Avoid touching the recording surface of disks, especially floppies, taking strict steps to prevent static electricity. Retain each disk in a protective sleeve when not in use. NEVER use paper clips and other fasteners in conjunction with floppy disks.

- Recommended storage conditions for this medium: 17-20 °C and 35-45% RH

Storage (General)

Materials of stable quality should ultimately be aimed for in storing personal papers and memorabilia. Documents can be stored in acid-free folders and artefacts in acid-free boxes. Acid-free boxes are reinforced by copper wire stitching, a very benign metal, giving the boxes great strength and durability.

- Although acid-free storage materials are more expensive than the standard packaging, they are a solid investment in determining the long-term preservation of family collections.

- Boxes of acid-free quality should have a close-fitting lid to ensure a stable climate in keeping out dust, light, pests and fluctuations in temperature and humidity.

- Containers should be designed to fit the object and not the other way around.

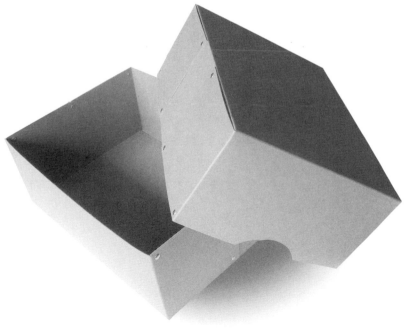

- To ensure that there is enough room for ventilation, do not over-fill boxes.

- Large format material should be stored flat and interleaved with strong acid-free paper. Portfolios should ideally be used for the storage of large maps and newspapers.

- Documents should be stored horizontally in acid-free containers rather than vertically.

- If oversize maps/documents cannot be stored flat, they should be rolled around a large diameter tube, covered with sturdy material and clearly labelled.

- Prints and drawings should have a window mount to protect them from physical and mechanical damage.

- Good quality materials should be used for mounting items. Artwork hinged to backboard is recommended, allowing it to hang freely in the mount and enabling it to react to changing atmospheric conditions.

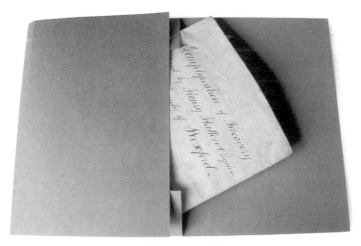

Processes used
Good or bad?

Reproduction

Laser copying provides an effective method of duplicating documents (photographs in particular) and can often produce a clearer copy than the original. It also significantly cuts down on over-handling of the original document. This process should ONLY be undertaken following an examination of the item in question and its ability to withstand copying, based on such factors as its condition and its vulnerability to light.

Laminating

Laminating should be avoided at all costs. This is a process where the document is embedded in plastic thereby permanently altering unique items.

Encapsulation

Encapsulation is generally not recommended as items can shift in their semi-permanent enclosure, thereby exposing the document to direct contact with the adhesive and accelerating its deterioration.

Digitization /Scanning

Digitization of materials, particularly photographs, provides safe and easy access to images in your collection. Once scanned, they can be viewed in electronic form and hard copies can be made without interfering with the originals. However, digitization should not be considered as a replacement for original documents, due to the dangers posed by technical obsolescence. *See also Electronic Records.*

APPENDIX 1

A short list of companies supplying archival quality products and materials is given below. Advice on purchasing the most suitable storage units for your collections should initially be made through an archivist. Generally, products must be purchased in bulk from suppliers and it may not be possible to obtain individual items. Inclusion in the list does not necessarily indicate the author's endorsement.

Advance Handling 2000 Limited,
Lower Dargle Road, Bray, Co. Wicklow,
Tel: (01) 286 7917, Fax: (01) 286 8005

The Paper Mill Company,
Woodview House, Stillorgan, Co. Dublin
Tel: (086) 266 7979, Fax: (01) 288 8748

Conservation By Design Limited,
Timecare Works, 5 Singer Way,
Woburn Road Industrial Estate,
Kempston, Bedford MK42 7AW,
United Kingdom
Tel: 0044 (0) 1234 853 555
Fax: 0044 (0) 1234 852 334
www.conservation-by-design.co.uk

Preservation Equipment Ltd.,
Vinces Road, Diss, Norfolk,
England IP22 4HQ
Tel: 0044 (0) 1379 647 400
Fax: 0044 (0) 1379 650 582
www.preservationequipment.com

APPENDIX 2

Useful websites to consult regarding the preservation of family materials:

National Archives of Ireland
http://www.nationalarchives.ie

National Library of Ircland
http://www.nli.ie

Public Record Office, UK
http://www.pro.gov.uk

Preservation of materials (general):

http://www.nedcc.org
http://www.oclc.org/oclc/presres
http://www.archives.gov/preservationb/index.html
http://www.statelibrary.vic.gov.au/slv/conservation/flatpapr.htm

Preservation of sound recordings:

http://www.audio-restoration.com/gilles.htm

Preservation of philatelic materials:

http://www.stamps.org/care/pcpm.htm

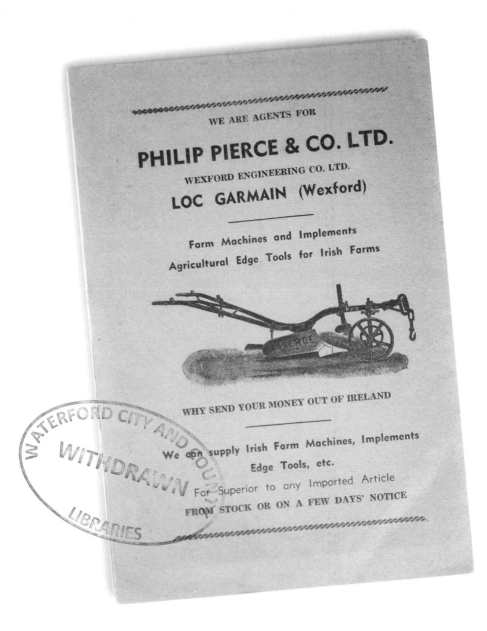